If Animals Could Talk:

# Cats

CURIOUS FOX BOOKS

ISBN 979-8-89094-054-4

Library of Congress Control Number: 2023943614

To learn more about the other great books from Fox Chapel Publishing, or to find a retailer near you, call toll-free 800-457-9112 or visit us at *www.FoxChapelPublishing.com.*

We are always looking for talented authors. To submit an idea, please send a brief inquiry to acquisitions@foxchapelpublishing.com.

Fox Chapel Publishing makes every effort to use environmentally friendly paper for printing.

Printed in China

If Animals Could Talk:

# Cats

## Learn Fun Facts About the Things Cats Do!

Cynthia Mead

When sunlight peeks through the curtain, I wake up because I am hungry. I need to wake up my friend.

I tap her with my velvet paw. "Wake up," I say, but it sounds like, "MEROWWWW!" She rolls over still asleep. I don't give up!

**Pet Fact:**

**Cats sleep up to 16 hours a day, but they can adapt to your schedule!**

"MEEP!" I say like a hungry kitten would to its mommy. When the message doesn't get through, I help myself by biting and scratching the bag of food. That works! She puts food in my bowl.

My eyes blink in love for my friend. We always have breakfast together, but her food smells different to mine. I am always curious about what she has!

**Pet Fact:**

**Long, low meows can mean your cat is angry. Shorter and higher meows are friendly.**

PROACTIVE HEALTH™
PROACTIVE HEALTH
Weight Control

After she dresses, my buddy says, "It's time for me to go to school. Bye-bye, Fluffy!"

I miss my friend. I will sit in the window to wait for her. But I also like sitting here to watch birds and other exciting things outside.

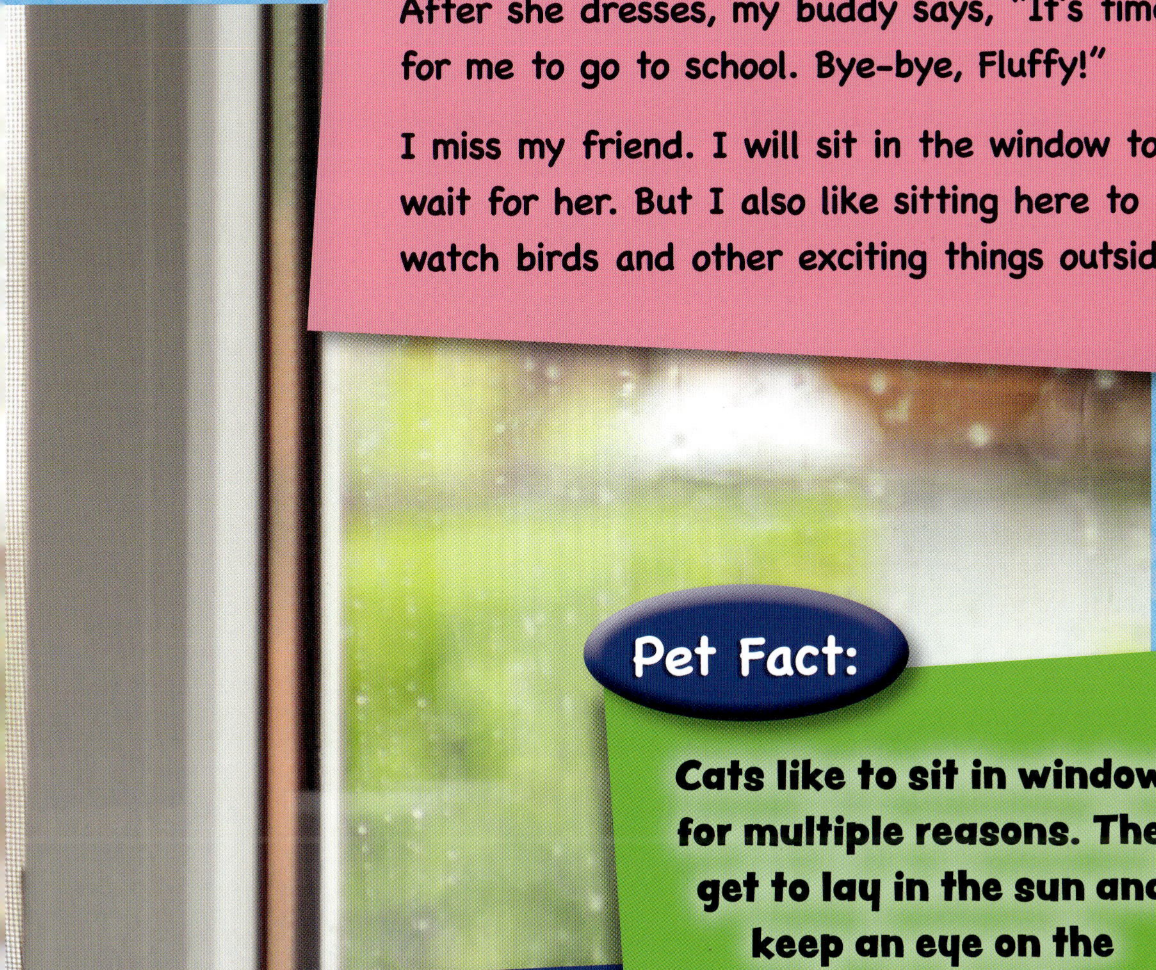

**Pet Fact:**

**Cats like to sit in windows for multiple reasons. They get to lay in the sun and keep an eye on the animals outside.**

Now its time to play with my favorite toy.

It really is amazing how it always waits for me to try to catch it, but I let it win sometimes, too. I can do this for hours!

**Pet Fact:**

**Cats often meow when they want attention, such as pets or playtime.**

Some early morning visitors drop by in the backyard. We try to touch noses, but that glass door is in the way!

**Pet Fact:**

**Cats touch their noses to people, animals, and objects to gather their scent. This is a way to find out who is a friend.**

I don't like having strangers in the backyard. I try to chat with them, but they don't speak kitty. Instead, I paw at the window, and they understand I want them to leave.

I dig my claws into my scratching post. When I do, I feel like one of my large, wild cousins! I pretend I am a tiger!

**Pet Fact:**

**Cats will scratch to leave scents that other cats can smell.**

After my workout, I'm still in the mood to explore. It's very easy for me to jump up on tall surfaces, even if my buddy says not to.

When I step on these funny white steps, they make music! Now I'm getting a little sleepy.

**Pet Fact:**

**Studies have found that music can calm and relax cats.**

OH NO! THE DOG! He heard me! I arch my back and stick out all my hair to look bigger. I twitch my tail because I am angry.

"YOWWWL!" I howl my feelings! "HISSSSSSSSSSSSSSSSSSSSSSSS!" That will show him who is boss!

**Pet Fact:**

**A cat's hiss is a warning to back away.**

Oh no, he's hugging me! And he licked me! That actually feels pretty good. I like getting groomed.

I lower my tail and relax. Maybe this dog and I can be friends, too.

**Pet Fact:**

**Cats groom each other to show that they are friends. When a cat licks you, they are saying that they like you!**

I'd better wash myself after that! There's nothing like a tongue bath to stay clean.

**Pet Fact:**

**Cats tongues are covered with papillae (tiny spines) that work like combs when a cat licks its fur. They feel rough if your kitty licks you!**

Time for my buddy to come home! Somehow I just know. I can hear the school bus way before it pulls up to our front door. I prick up my ears, and my tail stands straight up as a greeting.

I rub my cheeks on her ankles when she comes in the house because I love her so much.

**Pet Fact:**

**Cats mark you as their own by rubbing their cheeks against you with their scent glands.**

She takes a whiff of me, and the next thing I know, she plops me into the sink! Doesn't she know I just gave myself a bath? I guess I still smell like dog breath!

**Pet Fact:**

**Some cats hate baths, just like some kids. Let an adult help you bathe your cat so you don't get a scratch.**

Soon it's my buddy's turn, but she doesn't mind. She actually likes taking baths! I watch her carefully, though. Those little foamy things could swallow her up!

Later, she combs me gently from head to tail. This is nice. The next time I give myself a bath, I will get fewer hairs in my mouth.

Now it's bedtime. She pets me and I purr. I knead because I am happy. Right paw, left paw. Right paw, left paw. Velvet paws, no claws! I keep them tucked in.

I kiss her hand with a small lick. She says, "I love you, Fluffy." I say, "I love you, too," but it sounds like, "PURRRRRRRRRRRR."

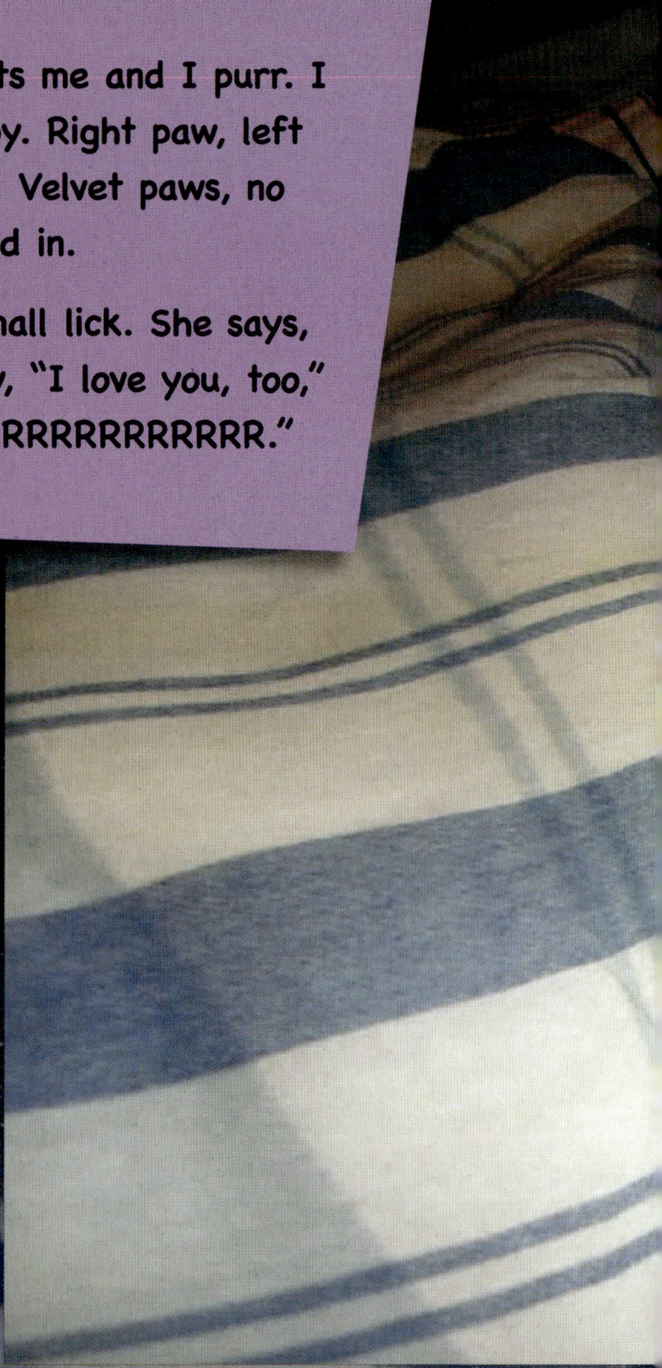

## BOOKS


Crisp, Marty. *Everything Cat: What Kids Really Want to Know about Cats.* Minnetonka, MN: NorthWord Books for Young Readers, 2003.

Farjeon, Eleanor. *Cats Sleep Anywhere.* Islington, London: Frances Lincoln Children's Books, 2010.


## WORKS CONSULTED


Gutman, Bill. *Becoming Your Cat's Best Friend.* Brookfield, CT: The Millbrook Press, 1997.

Hotchner, Tracie. *The Cat Bible: Everything Your Cat Expects You to Know.* New York: Gotham, 2007.

Johnson-Bennett, Pam. *Think Like a Cat: How to Raise a Well-Adjusted Cat – Not a Sour Puss.* New York: Penguin Books, 2011.

Nagelschneider, Mieshelle. *The Cat Whisperer: Why Cats Do What They Do – and How to Get Them to Do What You Want.* New York: Bantam Books, 2013.

Tabor, Roger. *Understanding Cat Behavior.* Devon, UK: David & Charles, 2003.


## ON THE INTERNET


CFA for Kids: About Cats
https://cfa.org/kids/

Kittenwar
http://kittenwar.com

National Geographic Kids
http://kids.nationalgeographic.com



PHOTO CREDITS: Shutterstock images: Nils Jacobi (1, 21 bottom right), Lena Miava (5 bottom right), savitskaya iryna (6 inset), Evgenia Terekhova (8–9), Kazbek Chermit (9 inset), rawcapPhoto (18 inset), PHOTOCREO Michal Bednarek (22–23), oes (24 inset), ANURAK PONGPATIMET (24–25), oksana2010 (32). Cover and remaining photos: CreativeCommons. Every measure has been taken to find all copyright holders of materials used in this book. In the event any mistakes or omissions have happened within, attempts to correct them will be made in future editions of this book.